I'M SORRY, YOU ARE NOT A PICK-UP ARTIST: A CHALLENGE YOUR SKILLS MANUAL FOR MEN

CREATED BY DR ETHAN GREGORY

EDITED BY DAWN HANSON

ETHAN GREGORY PUBLISHING

Copyright 2015 by Ethan Gregory

All rights reserved. In accordance with the US Copyright act of 1976, this book and parts thereof, may not be reproduced in any form without permission from the publisher; exceptions are made for published review excerpts. If you want to use content from this book, contact the publisher at drethangregory@gmail.com

Published by Ethan Gregory Publishing

www.drethangregory.com

ISBN: 978-0-9967819-6-1

Library of Congress Control Number: 2015915214

First Edition

Dedications & Acknowledgements

I have to thank James Bach. I began this book in 2006 while I was in between jobs and sleeping on his couch. My net-worth and self-worth were both at all time lows. His openness and generosity helped me rebuild a foundation in my life while I hustled to make ends meet. I have to give a shout out to Alina Reyes, the French erotica writer. After reading *Behind Closed Doors*, I saw the potential for having two narratives within the same book. Thank you for the inspiration, please don't sue me. Lastly, Ravishing Rick Rude, R.I.P. Your gimmick inspired me as an impressionable young man, and you are without a doubt one of the founding fathers of the EGA.

Table of Contents

Instruction Manual/Introduction	1
Chapter One	8
Chapter Two	14
Strip Club Choice	16
Local Choice	21
Chapter Three	33
Chapter Four	52
Trendy Choice	54
Hike Choice	60
Chapter Five	66
Chapter Six	78
Buildup Choice	86
Nature Choice	90
Raft Trip	95
Chapter Seven	111
Don't Stop Here!	114
About the Author	115

Instruction Manual/Introduction

I am aware that there are many different genders and partner preferences; please forgive me for not including more diversity in this edition. This book only has a cisgender man and woman protagonist. I do try to make neutral pronouns but I hope we can all enjoy the empowering lessons of the EGA regardless of our own identities.

If you have purchased this manual, then you are in for a special brand of advice from someone that has spent the majority of his life learning and testing out ways to succeed in building intimacy with the opposite sex. This guide is not just a tool for your sexual workbench; it will help you in your day-to-day interactions, creating a more confident and assertive version of yourself. The guide and interpreter for your voyage into the perilous territory of dating will walk you through the danger zones of interpersonal communication with womankind. Your guide will show you to the gates, yet you will decide at that point which way you continue. That is where you become the hero, and you practice the skills presented to you throughout the manual.

No one is expected to make the right choices every time. Dr. Ethan Gregory is there to dust you off and help you begin again. By making choices throughout the book, you save the precious pride and confidence lost by actually trying this out on a real woman before you are ready. When you make the wrong choice you will learn why, and we can hit the reset button. Next time, you will know the right choice to make. The summation of all these challenges is to create within yourself strength of character, and for you to know that if you hear a "no", it isn't the end of the world. Now that you know how the book works, I am going to share a bit of why the book works.

At age 16, I received a book in the mail entitled *SEX, a Man's guide*, written by Stefan Bechtel & the editors of *Men's Health* magazine. I had 21 days to read it or I had to buy it, and I didn't want to get caught with this book by my parents. I read it, sent it back, and realized that I wanted to help people with their sexual dysfunctions, relationship issues, and self-confidence. I dedicated my life to the cause. As a teen I learned how to flirt. I was perfecting a craft and experimenting with non-verbal communication techniques. At that time I was a virgin, and believed in true love, and wanted to wait until I met the right girl to have this romantic courtship followed by blissful lovemaking.

When the right girl was obviously taking too long, I set a time limit. I did not want to go out of the millennium as a virgin. I rightfully dumped the fairy tale, and adopted the reality that I was scared of commitment, my standards were too high, and I cared too much about what other people thought. At that point my life changed.

I became sexually active, and have been at various times single, committed, and contemplated marriage. I've had one night stands, weekend lovers, been asked to be a sexual boy toy for a gorgeous older woman, and experienced intimacy with both young and mature. The point of all my behavior has been to learn what it all feels like. Most of it was highly enjoyable, and some was emotionally painful. I pass on my knowledge to others.

I have gone down many wrong paths, made several bad choices, yet I achieve most of what I desire. The rejections in life were welcomed because the sooner I am rejected; the faster I am on to the next possible success. I do not let my quickcumings (I mean shortcomings) or disappointments bother me now. That lack of shame and optimistic perspective has benefited me in many aspects of my life. One of the more difficult lessons we will endure is to learn that one's rejection of us is not to be dwelled on.

My friends that know me well and witnessed most of the events I hinted at above created an acronym for the kind of behavior I exhibit, and the style in which I choose to lead my life. The term defines not just a fearlessness, lack of shame, disregard for consequences, or manner of carefree behavior. The term is used to explain a way of life, one where there are no restrictions placed upon oneself, and where success is judged not by achievement, but by merely attempting to achieve. This way of life is not for everyone; in fact it is not very safe for some people to try. By reading the book, you will learn to take on the positive characteristics of an ideal, to be your own Batman in a way, and that is the Ethan Gregory Approach, the EGA.

The EGA is built on the idea that we deserve to maximize our physical and emotional potential. This guide can help any man raise his standards and achieve a partner through no game playing, chivalry, and accountability. I have been deep in the game, and I have much to share with you about how to find the partner you are looking for. That said, if you have conservative views about gender roles, this might be a good time to pass the book on to one of your more modern-minded friends.

In case you were worried about the professional qualifications of your guide, I have a B.S. in Family and Child Sciences, a Masters in Clinical Social Work, and an Ed.D. in Counseling Psychology. I have worked in adult mental health providing therapy and suicide prevention, and I have worked in Child Protective Services trying to keep children safe from abuse, drugs, and neglect. I have studied in depth how people choose partners and which techniques are successful or not. I have had enough hands on experience in the game to not just beat the game, but like Jay-Z and Michael Jordan, I have retired from the game, come back, and owned the game. I have been reincarnated as your bedroom Buddha and I am here to help you achieve your own nirvana. Like Barry White said, "I can't lose with what I use". I am ready to pass on the techniques that help you throughout your interactions with the opposite sex. When you are ready to start, pack light. Shave your face, trim the man bush and Bic the balls, iron some clean clothes, and we will begin our quest.

Chapter One

Lighten Your Load

It's great to see you decided to take up the challenge. You are going to be experiencing a lot of new things. Before we get going, I need to know what you are bringing along with you. I see you have deodorant, underwear, two pairs of shoes and a belt, that's all well and good. If this isn't your first trip into enemy territory, you also have some castaways hiding in your pack. You have that emotional baggage from your previous relationships weighing you down. Before we go into the jungle, we are going to have to lighten your load a bit. Do you have a current partner? When was your last relationship? Put her name here_____.

Obviously you liked something about her, and were able to court her, knock her up; however you got her, you got her. What you have to do now is to try to overcome the negative feelings she created in you, thinking that you are not worthy of happiness with someone else. I too have had that emotional baggage, and I used to think that I didn't want to date anyone if it wasn't that girl. You may have yet to date anyone serious after her, and that makes it difficult to get back into the game, because your old memories and experiences create a cloud over you as you try and give the next girl a chance.

Dwelling on your ex is a great way to ruin your next relationship. If you are tying to get her back, then ok. But if your goal is to meet someone new, repeat after me. "My last relationship is over. I will never be with _____ again, because we would not have broken up if both of us wanted to be together." Now, maybe you got dumped, and you do want to be with your ex again. Let me just put this out there in case you have repressed it. If your ex really loved you, wanted you forever, lusted for you like a dog lusts for a walk, then guess what, stud? That's right, she would be with you.

People in our life become habits. We meet someone, and it is easy to not call them, even when they are excited about giving us their number. Why is that? They don't mean anything to us, that's why. It takes time to develop a relationship (habit of behaviors with the same person) and we become addicted to having that person in our life, hence the withdrawals after they are gone. So do you have this habit or addiction with your ex? It's time for your first exercise in the book.

We cannot move forward until you are ready 100%. That means setting yourself free from the past. I want you to go home, open up your closet, and take out the photo albums, the gifts, the shirts, the notes, whatever it is that you still have with her memory attached to it. You are going to say goodbye to it all. Most of what you kept, you don't even look at anymore, so just pile it all up.

Once you have it in a pile, get a bag, and put it all inside. I will leave exceptions for expensive items you use daily, a washer and dryer, that sort of thing. The pictures have got to go if they are with you and her. Exceptions can be made if the picture has a group, and one of them is dead now, unless it is the ex, the dead ex pictures have to go, unless you have a child together, in which case you are permitted to keep one picture on a mantle, and your child can have all the mommy pics they want in their room. Anything that you look at and see her is something that goes to the curb. You can burn it in a trash can fire if you want, throw in a credit card for good measure. However you get rid of it, just do it.

If you are at home, put this book down, and get to it. Do not keep anything in case she comes over sometime; remember that we no longer care about her opinion of us, or having her come over to shoot the breeze. If you still have some of her crap (shoes, clothes) then you are obligated to either mail it to her or arrange a switch. She may be holding on to your stuff as a trap to get you into her web. Do not sleep with her on this exchange, as this will lead to tears, cuddling and god knows what else. Exchanging stuff in public is best, got that? Good. Now that we have cleared our homes and our minds of our past relationships, we can begin the basic training.

Since you were allowed to pick out your first outfit, and what you wanted to eat at a restaurant, your life has been about making choices. Life is entirely about choices in the EGA. The choice to iron your clothes or not could be the factor that sways a woman to talk to you or not. The choices to bring up your criminal record or your addiction to World of Warcraft on the first date are choices that will affect your getting a second date. The life you lead now may be entirely kick ass, or it may be the life of a gaming geek. I am going to put your choice making skills to the test, and I'll be damned if you don't become a bit more bold in the process. Carry on friend, you are about to embark on a life changing adventure. Just keep an open mind and try to keep up.

Chapter Two

It's 5:00 Somewhere

After a hard day at work, you and your male coworkers are deciding if the group should go out for happy hour. You have nothing better to do, and you do not have anyone at home waiting on you since your relationship ended just one month ago. One coworker suggests the strip club. He is married, and that is the only place he ever wants to go. The other friend wants to go to the Irish pub for the drink specials. You know that there are plenty of women to look at in the strip club, but you went there last Friday night with the married guy and it is only Tuesday. The Irish pub does have good drink specials, but that is the place where you met your ex girlfriend, and you may run the risk of seeing her there. You haven't spoken to her since three weeks ago, when you exchanged each other's stuff. You got rid of everything that reminds you of her, (right?) and you have begun distancing yourself from the relationship. You love strippers, and appreciate the ego boost you receive while they say nice things about you during the pre "go to the back" stage. So what is it going to be? You are the deciding vote out of the group. Is it the dancers or the drafts?

To go to the strip club (of which you are three visits away from a tee shirt) turn to the next page

To go to the Irish Pub turn to page 21

Strip Club Choice

You tell your buddies that you are not ready to go to the Irish pub yet, but that you met a stripper last Friday and you want to see if she is there today. Your friends all meet up at Scarlett's and get your usual table (the one that sits far enough from the front so you don't have the pressure to tip, but towards the middle so you can see the girls in the back corner on the side stages). You talk over Patron shots and Coors Lights for a while, and you realize that your favorite girl is approaching the table. She sits down on your married friends lap and asks you about what you do for a living, and if you like Cuban girls. At that point you realize that the stripper doesn't remember you, and that the wonderful words and sweet-talking you did together meant nothing to her. Your married friend takes her to the back for a lap dance, and leaves you and your buddy to stare at the girl on the main stage spread-eagle sliding down the pole upside down. As your friend is buying another round with his credit card and talking about how much he would love to bone that girl, you realize that although you would do the same, you will never get that opportunity. The women in the strip club are there to work, not make a love connection.

Your money isn't enough to hold their attention. A skinny blonde girl in a schoolgirl skirt comes up to you and asks if you want a dance. You know that it is just a tease, but you say yes.

When you get home you rub one out, brush your teeth, and fall into bed, not caring that you stink like a bar, and you blew fifty bucks on a broad named Natasha. As you doze off you think to yourself that you probably should have gone to the bar, but now you are one visit closer to that free shirt.

So cowboy, you picked the strip club over the bar. That was a tough choice. There are plenty of reasons to not pick happy hour and go to a strip club, but I am only going to mention one. Did the fact that you might meet your ex at the bar sway your decision in any way? Both places have women, booze and entertainment. The Irish pub has become a symbol in your life, a place where something important happened. I can understand not wanting to go there. There is more work to be done with you before you are open to meeting someone new. You have to really cleanse yourself and your world of the memories you have of that ex.

I ate a great fish sandwich at a hotel bar in Beverly Hills a while back. That sandwich was the best damn sandwich I have ever had, hands down. I had to go back to that hotel for a show, but was I afraid of the fish sandwich being there? I had already come to terms with the fact that I ate the best sandwich of my life, and I may never have another that tasty and delicious ever again. I overcame my fear, and I know that you want to do the same. You must go to the places that you shared with a partner, and take them back.

Do not let her be the only one to enjoy a great meal at "your restaurant" or let her go to the park that you dirty dogs humped at after dark. This will be your next exercise. You are to reclaim all such places for yourself. What better way of putting old memories behind you, then to put some new ones in front of you? You are the man, baby! It's time that you understand that. You have got to begin to know that you are deserving of happiness, no matter what you did to someone else or what happened to you before you read that last sentence. As men, we seem to believe that we have to create some kind of pain, or make our life harder than it has to be, just to keep ourselves "hard" or undeserving. We have the right to enjoy life as an adult just as much as we did when we were children. My point is this- don't create emotional burdens where they don't exist. Sure, she was great. You may not have been. Maybe she was a cheating inconsiderate nag, and you did all you could because you loved her. That is not an excuse for beating yourself up and not striving to achieve happiness again. I have done it; we all have done it at some point. It takes baby steps, but that's why you are reading this, and that's what your boy is here to help with. So sleep on that "Mr. Singles" at the Gentleman's Club, and we can see what happens when we turn back time.

Local Choice

You tell your friends that you can't afford to do the strip club again, and that you are ready to baby step back into the single life. You and your married friend ride together, and in the car he tells you that he will be your wingman in case you need someone to fall on a grenade. You arrive at the pub to see that your buddy has three pints of the dark stuff waiting at a booth facing the bar. You slide in the middle, and take in the scenery. Your ex is not there, in fact, there aren't that many people there at all. The bar hasn't changed much since your last time in here with what's her name. The Golden Tee is a year ahead, but the music on the machine is still playing "Sweet Home Alabama".

As your buds are talking in front of you about wanting to have sex with the new receptionist, you notice that this is the time of year when the local university has just come back from summer. There are football schedules on the wall for the new season, and just below the poster for the girl's volleyball team, is a squad of pretty young women all huddled together at the bar. You survey the bunch. There is a tall blonde that looks like she could play on the volleyball team, two brunettes that look like twins but are probably just sorority sisters, and of course, the slightly unattractive red head with the freckles.

Your married friend taps your shoulder and says, "She looks like she belongs here." You know whom he is talking about, and give a head nod in agreement. You drink down the rest of your beer, and are feeling adventurous all of a sudden. You realize that you are in safe company with your friends. You take the opportunity to get a closer look at the girls and offer to buy the next round.

You shuffle your married friend out of the way and confidently walk up to the bar alongside the group of girls. You give a quick look back at your table and your boys are giving you smiles. You turn back around to ask the bartender for another round, and sit down on the stool next to the tall blond. You are too scared to look at her, but you can pick up the conversation from the girls. They are discussing the last episode from a popular TV drama. You know what they are talking about, because you and all your male co-workers are obsessed with the show, and you each have your favorite barely legal hottie that you love to watch.

The bartender returns with three full mugs and you tell the bartender to put it on your friends tab. You return to the table and tell your friends that they are talking about the show.

"I love that show!" states your single friend, and your married friend asks, "Are they married?"

You realize that you forgot to even look at the fingers to see if they had rings on. You say that you didn't look, and your friends exclaim their disappointment in your game.

Your single friend says that the two girls facing you were checking you out. You were too busy pretending not to care that they were there to make any eye contact. You can now see the group, and the girls have full martini glasses in front of them. You catch the eyes of the red head looking your way for a brief second, and then she turns her head back to her friends. From where you are sitting you can see the left hand of the red head, and there is a ring on the appropriate finger. "Red head's married," you report to the table.

All right my friend, let's assess this situation. We have you and two buddies, one of whom is married. There are three girls at the bar whose status is undetermined at this point. Maybe you are content to just ride out the next hour with your buds, and go home to jerk off and watch YouTube. You don't remember the last time you tried to approach a girl at a bar, but it's been a while. As a rookie, I can see how the situation is intimidating. As a veteran in the game, I can tell you that these are the best opportunities to test your confidence. With just a little bit of the EGA, you are going to be able to have your pick of the girls. This situation is more like playing chess, because it is about positioning and taking what the opponent gives you. Having your friends with you takes away almost all of the pressure on you to perform for yourself. If your friends are complete dumbasses, then this will not work, but you have great friends that are multidimensional and can carry on the conversation. (Right?)

This is a move that you will be able to use over and over to great success. The EGA requires bravery, and I will walk you through. You have to make the choice for yourself if you are going to be a leader or a follower. In the EGA there is but one choice. For better or worse, you will go first, because that is the only way to test yourself, and by you setting an example, your friends will also seek to be confident, and you will turn into a group of Casanova vampires having your way with hordes of women who will be helpless against your charm. So I give to you the mantra that keeps me ahead of the pack and pushes me to perform.

When I am about to do something I am scared of, like walking up to a bunch of beautiful women, or in the professional world when I would have to go up to the door past large barking dogs into a drug home to check on children's welfare, I say to myself "Indiana Jones would have done it". I think about Indiana Jones getting chased by that big ball, and he has to slide under the closing door before he is trapped. I force myself to go for it no matter the outcome. There is no shame in defeat, only in not trying. We are going in with the EGA, so the choice currently presented to you is this- which girl you want for yourself?

The girls are getting a bit louder as the volume in their glasses goes down. You see that the blonde and the brunette are chatting with each other, but one of them has their legs pointed in your direction. She is playing with the edge of her top and not making eye contact with her friend. She is giving you the non-verbal communication that says it's time to make your move. You tell your friend to slide out, that you need to use the restroom. On your way to the back, you make eye contact and smile at the girl you fancy. You pull up to the urinal, and start getting your words together. Wash your hands, and check yourself in the mirror. You look good. Thank god you ironed your shirt. Out the door, you pass the blonde as she is headed to the ladies room. You turn sideways in the hall to let her by, and as she passes, you say hello. She says hi and then ducks by. You walk up to the group of ladies, stand behind the red head and say in a confident voice with great posture:

"Hi, I couldn't help but overhear you talking about the show, what did you all think about the last episode?"

That should be all you need to get your foot in the door. The women will vocalize their opinions on the show; they may even ask you about your thoughts. Your next step is to introduce yourself. Tell them your name, and then ask the one that you like the most her name first. Repeat her name as she says it, and commit it to memory. Then ask the other women their names and commit them to memory too. You will use them later. As you greet the women focus your attention on the one you desire. The difference in what you would say before, and what you now choose to say is why you are going to have a date with this girl.

You are going to make a compliment about a physical detail or trait most people wouldn't. You are going to say that she has nice teeth if she does, or you find the scar on her shoulder cute. Use the magic triangle to focus your eyes from her ear, to her forehead, and across to her other ear. You won't freak her out with too much eye contact, and you won't take a peak at her breasts. When you have built some rapport with your favorite girl, excuse yourself and return to your friends.

You tell your friends at the table the names of each girl and report the details you picked up from your scouting expedition. Enjoy the rest of your beer and then round up the crew to join the ladies at the bar. When you come back to your girl, call her by name and ask her about her family or something from her past. Let her know about yours as well. This deeper level of sharing creates a stronger bond between the two of you. Use the 80/20 talk ratio. You talk 20, and she talks 80 percent. Her talking to you makes her feel more connected, and you reap the rewards. You tell her that you are normally a bit shy, but you had to take the risk of rejection to see if she was as interesting as you were pretending she was. Tell her that you would like to see her again and get her contact information.

Put her number in your phone right there and call it. If her phone rings, smile and be done. If it doesn't ring, smile and be done. She either likes you or she doesn't. Tell your friends that you are heading home for the night, say goodbye to each of the girls by name, and walk with confidence out of the door.

You are back in the saddle with the world at your fingertips. Resist the urge to call her tonight. Let your self wind down and marinate over the excellent work done at the bar. Let her think about the cool guy that charmed and entertained while creating a bond that makes her feel good about spending time with you again. You can't even remember why you hadn't gone to that place sooner than this night. The prospect of making such a great connection with a new person has swept away any remaining pain from your last relationship. You are once again on the prowl. This is not the time to get cocky and think that you can do this every night. You found a girl that gives you those goose bumps, and you need to see how this develops. The real work begins next day when you touch base with her and set up the first date. *Continue on to the next page.*

Chapter Three

Outside the Box

You are walking around the office with a bounce in your step today. Your friends are proud of you for making the transition from a wallflower to a brave participant in the dating economy. The small risk you took last night at the bar has given you a higher level of confidence that is lasting, not just one created by liquid courage. The time is right for you to challenge yourself. In the past, you may have waited a certain amount of days before calling a girl you are interested in dating. In the past you may have not called the girl at all because you were too much of a coward. Now that you have experienced the EGA to creating a peak introductory experience with a woman, you are ready to make the follow-up phone call. You can make many excuses as to why it is good to wait; building anticipation, you are not brave enough, or you never intended to call anyway. That kind of thinking has got you as far as you are now, which is nowhere. Let me let you in on a little secret. The girl you met last night, the one that was funny and sexy, that seemed so interested in your Skyrim character? She isn't sweating your phone call.

Right now you are just another man that she liked enough to give her phone number. You wouldn't be the first guy to wait a few days to call, and you wouldn't be the first guy to not call at all. Guys have created a pattern of mistrust and disinterest in beginning relationships with women. The stereotype of the girl waiting by the phone is no longer accurate. Your desired mate is going about her day as usual not giving you a second thought. This is why it is important that you create a pattern of reliability with her. You are going to be the kind of man that achieves all that he desires. On your lunch break you are going to call her and let her know that you enjoyed her company last night. You would like to set up a date soon with just the two of you. Be upbeat on the phone, especially if you get her voicemail. The goal of this conversation is to break the mold of her normal dating routine and to secure a future date. If it rings and goes to voicemail leave her this message.

"Hi __insert name here__ this is __your name here__. We met at the bar last night. I enjoyed talking with you and your friends yesterday and I would like to spend more time with just the two of us soon. Have a great day."

There is a lot more you may want to say to this woman. You want to tell her how hot you think she is, how you can't wait to be near her, and how you want to do her. That's all sweet and nice, but letting her know that doesn't help your situation. When establishing interest, you should be as succinct as possible. Tell the girl you are interested, but do not give out the dirty details. Let the girl use her imagination to develop those possibilities. She will be stunned that you called the next day. She will be relieved that you called (if she really likes you) and she will appreciate that you are honest enough to tell her that you enjoyed her and want more of her time. She isn't used to men keeping their word or being interested in her as an individual. By starting your relationship on a deeper level you will develop a deeper relationship over time. It will take less time to get her in the sack because you will have already put in the groundwork putting her mind at ease and building trust for you.

You took a big step by calling her while the conversation and chemistry is still fresh. It will serve you well to believe that you are not the only man seeking the attention of your potential mate. Creating a small sense of urgency will ensure that you devote the right amount of motivation and energy to achieving a relationship with her.

Now that the call has been made you can focus on your usual day-to-day activities. When you get home you are going to clean up your place. Now that you are back in the game it is time to play at a high level. The floor should be visible; the gunk on the tub floor should not. If it has been a while since you picked up a dust rag, pretend that you are moving out by the weekend, and you want your deposit back. You never know when you might be bringing someone back to the house so it's time to refresh your lifestyle as well as your kitchen. Pick a room per day and do the damn thing. Once it's done, you will feel accomplished. If you need to put the book down to begin the man-pad makeover then go ahead.

Now that the home is clean, we can focus on those details that you have been neglecting. How are your clothes fitting these days? I used to buy clothes a size bigger because I thought I would grow into them, now all my clothes are too big. Are you running out of belt loops for most of your pants? Do the necks of your shirts leave red marks on your skin because they are too tight? Do you own an iron?

These details are important because you are making a change in mind and body as you recreate the person you are into the person you want to become. Don't think that I am trying to change your character or your deep-seeded beliefs. I am going to assume that you are a great individual and the reason you have been slacking socially is a devotion to your fantasy sport team leagues and that you are ready to reengage with society, and in particular, with a woman. I am not going to tell you to change, just to clean up the person you are. That being said, lets evaluate your life up to now. How often do you work out or do any strenuous exercise? If the only exercise you get is when you masturbate, then that is a symptom of laziness. If you work out regularly it is a symptom of vanity, but the numbers don't lie. It is easier to attract a mate when you are attractive yourself. It really doesn't matter what you look like as long as you are doing good for you.

One benefit of being a man is that women have extremely low standards. You can get away with being out of shape as long as you make her feel valuable. The older she is the more out of shape you can be and still find happiness. That is a sad picture to paint of dating norms in our society, but I fear it is an accurate depiction. You bought this book, you are in the market for someone to share your life with (or at least new ways to screw hot chicks) so I want to invite you to utilize the days you have to make yourself the highest quality version that you can become. It will not only help you live longer and healthier, but it will make others more attracted to you physically and personally.

Trying to make another person like you will be hard enough without you not feeling good about yourself. If that means going to the gym, seeing a therapist, joining a team, then you do what you have to do. Make yourself ready to be loved and you will be ready to love another.

The woman that you met at the bar was digging you because you were the kind of person that you want to be all the time. One that speaks up for his desires and reaches for them is the kind of person that attracts others to them. You laid the groundwork with a great message letting her know that you desire her and her company. She feels complimented and interested in who you are. Let's call her again for the last time. As the man you have to assume that the woman will play hard to get and expect you to call, make all the moves, break your back for her attention. In reality you are a strong and proud man that doesn't make concessions.

When you ask for a woman's number you are creating a contract with her. You are letting her know that you are interested in doing business with her and that you are committed to being the one to initiate contact. For some men, collecting these non-binding contracts is fun and games. For you it will be a test of your honor and your fearlessness. You have called the woman once. You have initiated an exchange, but she will not always respond to this first contact. It was a sign of intention to leave a message, and it is always easier to leave a voicemail then to reach the woman directly. Your contract obliges you to make one additional effort. It won't hurt you any to try twice, and you will have done all you are obligated to do. If a woman does not call you back after two attempts, then she is in violation of the contract, and she can go to hell.

You have been waiting for your new lady friend to call you back all day and she has yet to return your call. You don't lose any sleep over this. You understand that things happen in life and messages don't always get checked promptly. You have entered the second day of knowing this woman and you are not going to let her rule your world. You have a busy workday to attend to. After winding down after work with your buddies at the strip joint, on your ride home you pull out your cell phone. "No new messages" says the voicemail woman. Now it has been 48 full hours since you met her, with no contact from her. It is time to man up and fulfill your end of the contract. You dial her number.

After the fourth ring she picks up, "Hello?"

"Hi this is <u>your name here</u> we met at the bar two nights ago."

"Right! I remember you. I didn't recognize that number. So what's up?"

All right Joe Cool; here is your opportunity to exercise your dating savvy. Use the following lines to write out what you would say to her during the phone call. You don't know how she is going to react, and you don't know what she is thinking. Just remember the EGA means leaving fear behind and openly stating what you want. (Hint: it's a date for this weekend) When you are done we can see the power behind the EGA and how it gets us where we want to be.

Ok young Jedi, did you use the force to get that date? If you let her do the talking then you allowed her to have the "hand" and that could mean she makes the decisions. Did you give a wishy-washy non-direct "maybe if you like me we can if you want go steady" kind of proposal? If you did it doesn't mean that you are a wussy, it just means that she now knows that you have trouble being assertive and that you are a pushover. If she likes dating pushovers, then you are in. I am willing to bet that she knew who you were the second the unfamiliar phone number popped up on her screen. I am also confident that she heard your first message and is excited that you called again.

When she saw your phone call, she waited four rings to compose her thoughts. She is not the only one that is nervous about talking to someone they find attractive. She may not be the coolest cucumber in the veggie bin either. She is playing her part as the pursued, and she is going to make you play hardball to get what you want. She is hoping you ask her out. She already cleared her weekend when you called her and stated your intention on the first phone call. All you have to do is pursue and she will be in hog heaven.

Here is how this phone call should play out. She says, "What's up?"

"I am having a busy but productive day so far, how are you feeling today?" You show her that you are ambitious and also not one that has time to waste in the day, making this phone call seem important, which shows her that you will accommodate her in your "busy" life. She doesn't need to know you were busy at the Gentleman's club. By asking her about her feelings first, not how her day was or something more superficial, you are getting her to open up and build trust as well as see you as a man that cares for her emotional well being. You do, right?

Listen to whatever she decides to say about her feelings, or her day, pay close attention. When she is done, no matter what she said you say, "It sounds like you really have it together." Women like to think that they know themselves really well, and they will accept this as a compliment. Take a mental note of what she said. If it was negative from word one, then that is probably the kind of person she is. If it was entirely positive, she is probably masking over some negative things for your benefit. Who goes through an entire day without feeling one negative emotion?

"I had fun with you at the bar the other night and I want you to join me for the day on Saturday or Sunday. Which of those is best for you?"

You bring her mind back to the good times you shared at the bar, putting her in a positive mindset for the question. Notice that first part is as direct as possible. There is no "would you like to" or "I would like it if" in the beginning of that statement. You are "all in" when you say something straightforward as "I want you to". That lets her know that you are taking a risk by letting her know that you "want" her to spend the day with you, not just a dinner or movie.

You throw her date expectations for a loop when you say that you want to see her during the day. Since the proposal is a direct one with little breathing room, you then allow her some control over the timing. You establish the ground rules, and give her the feeling of equal decision making. You are a team that considers each other's opinion. She will pick whichever day, and then she will ask what you have planned.

"I am planning a fun afternoon for the two of us, and all you will need are comfortable shoes. Do you have any allergies?"

Letting her know that you have something planned shows that you think ahead and that you are full of surprises. She will be guessing all week about what you could have in mind for the two of you. It builds anticipation. Telling her that she needs comfortable shoes is another curveball. She will want to get all gussied up for the date. No outfit will be super-hot in comfortable sneakers. You want to see her in the most natural form she will allow. Asking about allergies is being considerate and finding out how much of a freak she is. If she is allergic to everything, is that something you want to pass on to your possible children some day? Also, it lets you know what kind of foods she can't eat.

If she tells you that she cannot go this weekend then you have to ask her an important question. Let her know that you understand that this weekend is not good for a date, then ask her point blank, "Would you prefer me to not ask again? Do not add "it's ok if you don't" or anything else like that. Let her tell you directly that she is over it, or if she was just being friendly at the bar. If she says that she has a wedding or something else that cannot be missed, then you tell her this; "I felt something between us and I want to see you again, so let's keep in touch and you can tell me when a good day is for you. We will have fun whenever that is." Then it is time to get off the phone. Tell her that you are in traffic and want to be safe. Tell her that you hope she calls soon and to have a good night. Then it is on her to call you the next time, and you have created a new contract that will be up to her to keep or break.

In the meantime, you are not going to assume that she will call. You will go out with your friends and live your life as usual. You will not call her again until she calls you first. If she calls then great, if not then she has missed out an opportunity to change her life for the better by dating you. Her loss.

If she agrees to a day, then tell her that you will call her with details soon. Now, get off the phone. That is how you set up a first date without wasting any energy. You have implanted many good things during the phone call, some she will not recognize because they are in her subconscious and you never said them directly. If your written conversation was anything like that, then you are doing well for yourself. If it was the opposite of that then we have some work to do to get that tongue sharpened. Now that we have taken ourselves out of this girl's dating cookie cutter we are free to create the kind of relationship we choose, starting with the first date.

Chapter Four

Searching for Clues

This has been a busy week for you, and it should feel great. You have worked hard, met a great girl, and now you have something to look forward to this weekend. Have you been doing your homework? Is the house getting clean? Are your health goals progressing? You are an ongoing project that may never have an end date, but needs to be worked on each day.

The time has come to create a plan for your upcoming date. What are you planning to do? You have asked your friends that are in relationships for some good advice on places to take your honey and they have given some suggestions. Your married friend tells you that he had a good meal in the new café downtown last week. The menu was low priced and the atmosphere was lively. The health nut in the group tells you about a great hiking trail about five miles outside of town that winds around a lake that would be good for a picnic. You check the weather report for the weekend and it shows that there is a fifty percent chance of rain. Today is Thursday and your date is on Saturday. You are obligated to give her the 48-hour notice as a minimum level of respect. You make your choice, pick up the phone, and call her up.

"Hello?"

"Hi <u>insert her name</u> it's <u>insert your name</u>. How are you feeling today?

She says "blah blah blah".

"I wanted to confirm our date on Saturday and let you know what we have planned. We are going to…"

For the fun lunch date at the new café turn to the next page

For the scenic lake picnic date turn to page 60

Trendy Choice

You sit patiently waiting for a table with your date outside of the new café. It is a warm day, and you are starting to get swamp-ass in your khakis. The hostess finally calls you into the restaurant after thirty minutes. Inside, the place is bustling. You are given the table directly in front of the bathrooms. You would ask if you can have another, but that would mean more waiting. You are a gentleman so you give the woman the view of the restaurant. This happens to put you face to face with the television on the wall, which is displaying a sporting event on ESPN. There is music throughout the café, some kind of foreign language that is just loud enough to make it difficult to hear what your date asks you. You order light after your date decides she wants the most expensive appetizer and entrée. She looks great, and you tell her so. She says thank you, and begins to explain how she picked out the outfit she was going to wear. Throughout the meal, you constantly have to repeat your questions over the music, and remind yourself to keep your eyes off of the television and her tits. As lunch is wrapping up, you throw out the idea of catching a matinee at the movies. She agrees. You catch the 5:00 showing of "Sob Story 3" because she didn't want to see an action movie and you already saw the comedy.

During the movie you try not to fall asleep while she bawls her eyes out. You two head back to your cars, discussing why the lovers had to die at the end. The night ends with a hug and a kiss on the cheek outside her vehicle. As she pulls away you tell her that you will call her soon. You get in your car and drive home to jerk off and go to bed. As you lay awake thinking about the date, you realize that for spending an entire day together you learned nothing about your date. You spent a lot of money on a meal and a movie, but you feel like there wasn't a great opportunity to get to know her better. Maybe you could have asked her to join you for a drink after the movie let out, but she was in such a terrible emotional state that you just wanted to get away. As you doze off, you commit to calling her and setting up another date so that you can ask all of the questions that you meant to ask today.

The first date is always a nervous endeavor for both parties. When you are meeting someone for the first time (besides being drunk at a bar) it requires certain skills. When you are on the first date, it is important to bring your tool belt. You are going to need to have your listening ears with you to pick up the details that make up her preferences. The questions you ask are geared to get information to use on the future dates to come. Think of yourself as the interrogator and she the prisoner with information about a top-secret plot. By engaging her with open-ended questions and building the rapport and comfort between yourselves she will let slip some confidential information for you to use against her in the future. In order to gather the information you have to be in a place that will allow for the best listening possible. A noisy café is not the ideal location for such a mission.

When you sat down to eat you let her have the view of the restaurant which I have always been told is a gentlemanly thing to do, yet you were set up for failure having a television with a sporting event to look at. On any date you should never give yourself access to anything that might distract your eyes from the face of your date. In this case it might have been better to let her face the TV. The café was too noisy to do any productive listening, and you can't build rapport and intimacy when you can't listen to what she says. I understand that there was no way to know that going into a place for the first time, but then you decided that it would be a good idea to see a movie after lunch. That was not a good idea. When people go to see a movie on a first date it is a comfortable choice. There is no talking during the movie so no one has to be nervous about saying something stupid. For you, as an explorer of new people, it does not serve your purposes well. If the movie sucked, then you risk being associated with a bad experience. When choosing initial experiences with a new person you need to make the events useful to the overall mission, which is to gather intelligence. Any event that distracts your date from you or creates negative feelings is a bad date option, at least in the beginning stages of a relationship. You might have had a great meal and seen a great movie but you did not have a productive date. If your goal is to increase intimacy, you are now one date behind schedule if she wants to go on a second date. Do you pay for everything on the date? Did she offer to split any part of the movie or meal? How you use your money is completely up to you but take note- if she doesn't even offer to cover her own expenses, she may be inconsiderate. For an alternative to the meal and a movie date see what happens when we take the first date outdoors and out of the comfort zone.

Continue onto the next page

Hike Choice

It's Saturday morning and you are putting the lunch packs in a safe container for your outdoor excursion later in the day. You let your date know that you are taking her to a scenic area for a hike and a picnic lunch. You know what she does and does not eat because we cleared that up on our pre-date phone call. For the first date you have picked up lunch from a quality restaurant that makes packed lunches and you stopped by the store to get a bottle of wine. You have water and a blanket at the ready. When you arrive at your date's house you get out and ring the bell. She comes out to greet you and you open the door for her to get in your vehicle. You close it after she gets in. As you go around to your side, see if she opens your door from the inside or even attempts to reach. If she does, you know she is considerate and if she doesn't, try not to hold it against her.

You let her know that you have everything needed for the day and ask if there is anything she needs to pick up for a day outdoors. You travel to the park where you will be hiking, and along the way you ask detail oriented questions with the radio on low or not on at all. She fills in her various likes and dislikes about foods, flowers, and ice cream flavors. You discuss how your respective weeks went, and the details of your jobs. You begin your hike around the lake with no one else around.

The weather is great, and the two of you take in the nature around you, building up a sweat as you venture up and down hills overlooking the dark water of the lake below. When the bugs begin to bite, you are there with the bug spray, showing that you plan ahead, and that she can trust you to provide for her safety. You reach a soft patch of grass and tell her that you think that this is the spot to have your picnic. You lay out the spread and the two of you indulge in the meal. You talk about her childhood and long-term goals that the both of you have for your lives. You are repeating some answers back to her, acknowledging her feelings, telling her that you are glad she accepted to meet with you, and that you appreciate her adventurous spirit. You are creating rapport and intimacy by using communication skills.

By taking her on an active date you engage her hormones, raising her testosterone, initiating her sex drive. She is appreciating the outside the box approach to a first date. After lunch, you hike back to the car. By trail's end you are holding hands and very pleased with the day. As you drive out of the park, she suggests that you take her home so that she can change clothes and then meet for drinks.

When you drop her off you tell her that you know a quaint spot where the two of you can get a meal and the drinks are strong. She knows the place and you meet for an early dinner. The atmosphere is great for talking, there is soft jazz playing in the background, the lights aren't so dim that you can't see her, and when the waitress comes over your date asks for separate checks. You reflect on your hike and the things that you saw along the way. You let her know that you think she looks fantastic. You ask her about her hair and she goes on for minutes about different styles and cuts she has had while you pretend to be interested.

You eat, drink, and are merry together having a fun time talking and learning about one another. You tell her that you have had a stimulating day with her and that you look forward to another date soon. She agrees. You pay your tabs and as you exit the establishment, you give her a kiss on the lips. You thank her for giving you her number at the bar earlier in the week. After walking her to her car, you tell her that you will call her soon. You go home and jerk off, knowing that you have planted the seeds for a relationship to grow. You have gathered lots of information to set up a productive second date. If you need to, write down the details that you learned so that you don't forget. Every interaction that you have with her builds on the last one.

You are not in a rush to sleep with her, and you make sure not to come across as desperate for sex during the date. Rest assured that she went home and called her girlfriend or her mom and talked about the interesting date she just came home from. You were attentive and prepared, providing a quality experience for her. She is intrigued by your style and your creativity. She is hoping for another opportunity to explore what you have to offer. You are in the driver's seat cruising the fast lane to her mind and body. The next date will put the reconnaissance done during the first date into action to create an experience that she will not be able to resist. By now you have cleaned every room in your house and by the beginning of the next date you will need to wash your bed sheets (or get new ones if the stains don't come out). You are enjoying the benefit of being adventurous, outgoing, and prepared. You have a potential partner right where you want her. She is impressed with you and the EGA will continue to work as long as you stay true to the principles.

Chapter Five

Be the Broom and Sweep Her Off Her Feet

You tell your friends about the weekend you had and give the details of your date. They are impressed that you were able to pull yourself together and they are jealous that now you are the one having the success with women they always wanted. You should be proud of yourself for making the changes in your life that have allowed you to devote your energy to the future, instead of dwelling on your past or present. Of course your friends ask if you slept with her, but you let them know that it wasn't even on your agenda for the weekend, and if it was it just might have happened.

They laugh at your cockiness but you saw the moments that your date was hinting at something more, making herself available to be taken in her subtle gestures to spend a bit more time together after your drinks and dinner. Was it a guaranteed lay? Not by a long shot, but there was opportunity to advance past what you did, and that is what makes you a gentleman. By respecting the innocence of the first date you have set yourself up for the payoff coming soon. A woman might be testing your ability to restrain your primal urge to devour her, and just because she puts out a little bait, doesn't mean that you are to fall into the trap.

You were right to bend the rule on the first date by giving a spontaneous kiss on the lips, which showed your passion without creating discomfort about you being a pervert. You already know that the girl wants to sleep with you because she accepted a date in the first place. It's up to you not to blow your chance before she is ready to give it to you. She wanted to do you after the date, but she has her stereotypes of being a good girl, not looking like a slut to you, or to her girlfriends the next day. I am not saying that sex on the first date is a deal breaker for a relationship, but you know how you feel right after you have sex with someone you just met, like you have no use for that person anymore. That is why I advocate for holding out until an emotional bond is formed. There is too much natural instinct to hit and run in us to try and fight that urge without a bond created between you and the girl you really like.

By keeping it limp you won't make it hard on yourself. Desire is a strong emotion, and it will work in your favor when you question if the wait is worth it. If you are using your penis to look into a woman's heart and mind then you will be disappointed. Your penis has just one eye, and looking at some of our past partners, it doesn't see that well.

What did you learn on your date? Do you remember everything that she said about her likes and dislikes? The time you spent digging for details will serve you well on the next date and in the future. It is impressive to a woman when you recall something she said in passing. The next date will be the accumulation of the work you have put in. You are taking the date into your territory. You are going to create an experience that will prove that you are interested in your sweetheart for more than just a brief affair.

The cleaning up and the updating you have done to your home will play a part in the experience. You are going to prepare a full meal, and if you are lucky she will give you the dessert that you have been waiting for. Now that you understand that communication and keeping yourself fresh in her mind is important to maintaining a positive reputation, you are calling every 48 hours to chit chat and you have planned ahead by letting her know that the next date will be more relaxed and that you are going to prepare the meal in your home. Letting her know that ahead of time will allow her to reduce the anxiety of coming over to your home for the first time on short notice. When you suggest that she should bring a bottle of wine that she has never tried, it gives her a chance to own the date and play a role in the preparation, keeping her mind on you and your combined future.

You are going to prepare something that she said she likes on your first date. There are no rules, if she says that she loves hot dogs, then lucky you. If she said she loves steak and lobster then you might need to put some extra hours in at work, or you can go for something else she said she liked. Remember her allergies and food limitations. If she is on a low sugar diet, don't bake bread. She is expecting you to be cooking and slaving over the kitchen, but that doesn't have to happen if you are not culinary competent.

On your first date you talked about favorites, her favorite dessert should have come up. If the hardest thing you know how to cook is toast, then here is an equally fun alternative to impressing her with what you can cook. The day before your date (prior planning prevents piss poor performance) you are going to collect all of the favorite sweets and desserts that your honey said she liked. If she named three kinds of cake, ice cream and candy, then get what you can get. Bring them home and have them at the ready.

Netflix a DVD or download her favorite movie or if you asked about it, see if you can get a copy of her favorite show she watched as a kid (torrent it if you are on a budget, let's not be wasteful). I think somewhere after college years "watching a movie" becomes code for and background noise for sex. If she already watched the movie, she won't be too concerned with the plot, and if it is a romantic comedy, you are pretty much in, but this doesn't have to be the first time. Like meeting a new dog, you have to let it smell your hand before you try to pet it. Let her feel your home is a safe place, and she will not be worried that you might be an axe-wielding rapist.

One hour before your date, call and order a pizza (a small pizza) with the toppings she said she liked. Put the oven on warm and keep the pizza in it. Make sure that the place is spotless and light a scented candle to mask the man odor that permeates your home. Take some Gas-X. She will come over expecting a fine meal because that is what you told her you were going to make. When she arrives greet her and show her around the house. When you are ready to eat take out one of the lighter desserts and call it the appetizer. For the main course you are to bring out the heavier desserts, and for dessert bring out all the rest. Sit and enjoy the movie together and have fun pigging out on sweets. If at the end of the night the two of you are still hungry you have the pizza to eat.

When she is high from the wine and on a hormone rush from the sweets and chocolate she should be putty in your hands. Once again you have thrown her for a loop. Instead of the typical badly cooked meal and a movie you have taken her details and created an outside of the box exciting night full of good feelings and fun memories.

She sees that you listened to her and that you are able to have fun and break convention by having an all dessert dinner. She may be taken aback, but she won't be able to resist the childlike fun of having dessert for dinner and watching the old shows. Engaging her inner child will bring out her playfulness, and take her back to a time when her desire was her only motivation, before she learned that indulging is a bad thing. She will be impressed, and you will reap the rewards. She may want to sleep with you at this point, and you are free to oblige that request as long as you have protection.

If you do have sex, you need to have a short conversation with her afterward. Before you fall asleep, make sure to tell her that you were nervous about having sex with her so soon because you didn't want to scare her off or make her feel uncomfortable. No matter how long you waited to have sex, that line is great for making her feel that she made the right decision in sharing her body with you and will pretty much guarantee you get to do her again even if everything went wrong in the bedroom. After sex she is the most vulnerable to second guessing her behavior. By showing some insecurity it will validate her feelings. You can ask her if she wants to spend the night and offer her some comfortable sleep clothes if she says yes.

Otherwise, walk her to her car and give her a strong hug and kiss goodbye. Thank her for trusting you enough to come over to your house, and tell her that you think she is great. Put her in her car, and go back in the house before you start shouting in success. Yes, you are the man, but she doesn't need to see you jumping for joy in her rear view mirror.

If you happen to be a great cook, by all means prepare to your hearts content. The result will more than likely be the same as long as you cater to her needs and ensure that you utilize the details that she gave you. It's a good thing to keep a new toothbrush in the bathroom just in case she stays the night. She won't think anything of it, and it will eliminate a small excuse for why she wouldn't stay over. One thing to keep in mind is that sex is not the goal of the date, nor is it the sole reason you are entertaining this woman.

The only goal you should have in your mind is to learn about the other person. As an expert on sexual motivation, I find providing experiences that create intimacy and excitement with a woman will make her inhibitions disappear and she will feel comfortable sooner than she intended because it will feel like a natural progression in her mind, because you are in her head pulling the strings that control the puppet. If she doesn't want sex after the second date it doesn't mean you are doing something wrong. After her friends hear about the night you created for her they will be telling her to sleep with you, because they hear how you are attentive and creative. It's only natural to believe that will translate to when you are lying down. Feel confident that you are doing everything that you can to be in the right place at the right time. It's up to you to be ready when your number is called.

Chapter Six

Batter Up

Your days seem to fly by at work. You are seeing your girl once a week and going through the motions of courtship. You are always learning more and storing the information for later. You have kept your relationship with your friends up as well, going out with them during the week and talking the naughty guy talk, flexing your new EGA muscle when you see a hot chick that you want to talk to. Practice makes perfect and the fact that you have a good girl in your back pocket makes it easier to approach strangers.

Your friends are now asking you for tips on how to approach women, and the feelings of success are contagious. Even the married friend is joining in the action, even if it is just to see if he still has his mojo. You have met a few other girls out for drinks or lunch, you even scored with a girl from a college nightclub that your married friend took you to. It was nice to experience someone new that you didn't care a thing about, but you couldn't help but think about your shorty after the girl left your apartment. You have moved onto the bases but you have yet to hit the home run ball. You can tell the tension is there for the both of you.

All signs are leading to the holiday weekend coming up. She told you that she wants to get out of town for a weekend back on your first date, and you have been waiting to see how the relationship developed to put a plan into action. With an extra day off you have begun to discuss with your single friend the best option for a weekend getaway that will ensure that you come home satisfied and successful in having that first time sex.

"I once went to the beach with a girl, and the car ride ruined the entire trip for us. We got into an argument within the first half hour of a three hour trip, and we both agreed to turn the car around."

Your friend goes on about how his date couldn't make a decision on where to stop for lunch and that it infuriated him enough to completely cancel the trip. You thought about maybe driving out to the country for a wine tasting trip and staying at a bed and breakfast for the weekend, but now that was sounding like it could go bad quickly.

"My wife and I just went on a weekend cruise to the Bahamas," the married guy interjects. "We had sex all day long and got completely wasted every night. It was a blast until my wife had diarrhea and puked in the cabin bathroom. I couldn't breathe. I had to go up to the top deck for two hours while she blew up the bathroom."

A cruise does sound like a fun idea, but you don't want to spend that kind of money and god forbid that happen to you, there would never be any sex. So what could you plan for the upcoming weekend? Something here in town, an excursion out of town, or ask her what she would like to do? Take a second to think about it and write what you would do for the holiday knowing that your goal is to have fun and have sex.

_____

_____

_____

The holiday weekend is a great excuse to make a destination trip. An extra day allows for travel time and some prior planning can create an adventure that the both of you can enjoy. Remember those details your girl told you about, that she always wanted to do? Did she ever mention a place she hasn't been, or maybe something she was scared to do but always wanted to try? Does she like to get all gussied up and go out on the town? Is she a laid back, enjoy the scenery type girl? Use the intelligence that you gathered way back when.

    The first thing you need to do is tell her not to make any plans for the weekend to guarantee that she knows it is to be spent with you, and for good measure, I would throw in that you want this weekend to be especially memorable. That will get her and you on the same page, that sex will be a part of the activities. You now have to create an itinerary that she will approve of. Give her two options and make sure that she picks one of them without deferring the choice to you. Begin the reserving of rooms and preparing the most important part of the trip, you sharing intimacy with her.

She tells you that she would like to take a trip to the country to go wine tasting. You know of a really old bed and breakfast in walking distance of a winery. You book a room for the last night of your trip. For the excitement aspect, you contact an outdoor adventure place along the river and reserve a whitewater-rafting trip for the day, and a cabin at the rental site. The plan is set in stone, and you have the makings of a great weekend. There is balance in the events with a bit of lazy fun, and a bit of an adrenaline rush. What you need to do now is plan the details that are going to ensure that no matter what happens along the way, you are still going to have the result you want at the end. Call the B&B and have your girl's favorite flowers delivered in the room before you get there that day; if you don't know, get tulips and sunflowers. Tulips are pretty and phallic, and they have a higher "cool" factor than generic roses. Contact the winery, find out how much the wines cost and prepay for a bottle of wine. Your honey will be pleasantly surprised that she gets a "free bottle of wine" and people are usually game to play along when they know you are doing something special for another person. Remember, prior planning prevents piss poor performance. The EGA is details oriented. The big things are what she will enjoy, but the details are what she will brag to her friends about.

The car ride out to the river goes well. You ate before you left, and you had her bring her cd's to ensure that she has something she likes to listen to as well. The cabin is not as rustic as you were hoping, but she seems relieved. There is running water, but little twin sized beds. Despite having dated for a while, you have never spent the night together.

The rafting trip leaves early in the morning, but you have time to kill. Is it time to push those beds together? Maybe you can venture out into the woods and be one with nature while you do the wild thing.

There is no one around, and there is nothing but peace and quiet in your environment. Being away from the city has taken away any stress from work, and you can see your girl beginning to relax as well. You are suddenly feeling frisky being alone with your date in a new place. She is thumbing a brochure for the trip and giving you that look you saw from the girl in the club right before she went down on you on the car ride home. What are you going to do?

To take a walk on the wild side turn to page 90

To let the tension build up to a boil, continue to the next page

Buildup Choice

Knowing that you could do something doesn't mean that you should, especially when there is so much more planned for the weekend. To blow it early, literally and figuratively could ruin even the best-laid plans. You brought some beers and food to cook over the fire and now is a great time to start one up. You walk outside to the fire-pit and stack the wood. By the time the fire is blazing, the sun has gone down. The food cooks as you and she watch the flames and sip the IPA. The fire creates an atmosphere of intimacy; the cool wind makes it feel right to cuddle close.

After your meal and s'mores there is a buzz in the night and in your head. As the fire dies down you are making out and hands are wandering. You know she is digging the manly man that creates fire and food with his hands and is now cupping her breasts through that flannel button down she has on. You and her rise and return to the cabin. You see the time is late, and you know that you have a hard morning. You are of strong mind and body although you are also half-aroused and could be ready for action at any moment. You tell her that she is making it hard to be a gentleman and that you find her extremely hard to resist.

You go upstairs and drag the twin mattresses to the living room. You put them together and tell her that before you "sleep" with her you want to sleep with her. You bring out your laptop, throw on "Deliverance" and set it up so you can see it from the floor. The two of you cuddle up on the makeshift bed and hands roam until you fall asleep after the movie ends.

You made it to the morning and you have your dignity intact. You are on schedule with not only your trip, but also getting her so wound up that there will be no controlling her by the end of the weekend. She feels the desire that you feel, but you have to know that she may have apprehension about being alone in a cabin with a man, and she probably needed a night of trust building and comfort in close space with you. It will pay off soon. If things had gone all the way, it doesn't mean that it wouldn't work out well, but if it didn't then you would be stuck with reservations for two more nights and a frustrated woman to deal with for 48 more hours.

A night of cuddling skin to skin and showing restraint lets her know that you are a man that respects the cuddle, and will not poke her with your penis until she gives in. Just because she doesn't hand you a number two pencil doesn't mean that she isn't testing you. With each new physical milestone you have to be mindful of respecting her body. She is expecting you to test boundaries because that is what she is used to with the men in her past. As you are transforming her precognitions of what a man does, you are building yourself up as unique to her, and the respectful man gets way more unsolicited head then the disrespectful horn-ball (trust me).

To start your rafting trip and float through your weekend turn to page 95.

Nature Choice

When you see that look in your girl's eye, you ask her if she wants to take a walk in the woods. She says "Sure!" and grabs two beers from the cooler. The path into the woods is clearly defined in the cabin floodlights. As you venture a bit into the thicket you can barely make out the path in front of you. You hear the rolling gargle of the river ahead and you reach the water's edge to find a clearing that will suit your needs.

You turn to your girl and scoop her up in a kiss. You and her find your way against a tree trunk and are making out with urgency. She gets her hair caught on a piece of bark and you pull her away from the tree and lay down in the clearing. She finds her way on top of you, and you are unbuttoning her flannel shirt because it is vital to see and touch her breasts at this moment. She helps you slide her shirt off her shoulders and her body glistens in the moonlight reflection from the water.

You work your way into a spider position as she rips your shirt up and over your head. With her butt resting on your thighs you have roaming hands from the front to the back to the butt to her face, caressing and touching everywhere at once. Your mouth reaches her bra and you use your teeth to pull down one side revealing the upper portion of her breast. You kiss and peck around the area and return to her face to mouth kiss her. She has her hand up the leg of your shorts and is rubbing over your cock with her hand, forcing you to bulge through your briefs. The moment seems perfect and you are full-steam ahead. She asks if you have a condom.

"Um… yes, I do but it is back at the cabin," you say, trying to play it off quickly.

"Well it's ok, I am on the pill," she says without hesitation.

You pull off her bottoms and toss them aside revealing a lime green thong and a small tattoo of some kind of animal that you can't make out in the dark. As you take a moment to think about why she is wearing a thong on a camping trip, a rustle in the bushes startles the both of you. Your girl grabs her shorts and rolls around behind you. You can't see anything but you see the bush rattling around. You are trying to act cool as you back slowly up to the tree. A raccoon barrels out of the wood and into the clearing with you. Your date is already up and around the other side of the tree as you jump to your feet. The raccoon walks up to the water and you see him look you in the eye.

"Get my shirt," your girl says as she creeps backward up the path. You keep an eye on the raccoon as you inch closer to the shirt, equidistant between you and the rodent. You and the rodent are having a staring contest. It takes a step towards the shirt, and you take a step back.

"Be careful," she whispers at you from a safe distance, "It might have rabies."

You circle around to the water and splash up some water at the raccoon. It scurries off into the brush and you quickly grab up yours and hers shirt and meet her on the trail.

"Let's get back to the cabin," you say as you hand her shirt to her and you pick up the beers. The walk back to the cabin doesn't take as long as the walk to the water, you and her are double-timing it to the lights and safety of the indoors. You and her crack open the beer and laugh about the close encounter with nature. You decide to stay inside and watch a movie on the laptop while you heat up some hot dogs on the grill. You watch "Deliverance" together enjoying the food, beer and each other. After the movie you head to the beds, but there is too much sexual tension looking at each other from across the tiny room to get a good sleep. Eventually you doze off.

Raft Trip

The morning strikes you in the eyes as you attempt to avoid the glare coming through the window. After last night you know that your plan may come to fruition. You are the first out of bed. You put the coffee on and whip up some eggs and toast. As your baby begins to stir, you watch carefully. You never interacted with her in the morning and you are curious to see how she is in her natural form without being all gussied up. She turns to watch you, but does not get out of bed.

You trade good mornings and as the coffee percolates she slowly rises from the floor, wearing a little spaghetti string camisole and boxer shorts that could have belonged to an ex-boyfriend, which turns you off a bit. She isn't a monster in the morning, and she comes to join you after returning from the bathroom. You reminisce about the night before and voice your anticipation for the trip ahead. A shower would be pointless since you are about to be tossed about in a freezing cold river. The two of you head to the bedroom where your clothes are stored. You are not shy, and you disrobe in front of her to put on a swimsuit.

You do not delay in your changing, but you catch your girl turn her head around as you come to face her. Maybe she was checking you out. You tell her that you will wait in the kitchen for her to be done changing. It is acceptable for you to disrobe in front of her because you are showing that you are comfortable with your body, which will in turn allow her to be comfortable with your body and model for her that she should feel the same in her own skin.

By excusing yourself, you give her the respect of privacy, and also the opportunity to tell you not to leave, empowering her to make decisions about her comfort level with you and herself, something you should be taking notes on. The two of you arrive at the rafting center and put on your silly overall-looking wet suits. You have your waterproof camera on a neck string, and you take a picture of your girl all bogged down with gear. The other people in your raft seem friendly enough and you want to sit in front of the raft because that is what the EGA tells you to do; face challenges head on.

You defer the front spot to the teenage son of another couple in your raft to sit alongside your date, the tactful and smart thing to do. Having you be ahead or behind her would create two different experiences on the same trip and you want to have as close to the same story as she does, to create a symmetrical memory of the weekend. That is what builds closeness and intimacy.

The trip takes you through beautiful lush woods, fierce rapids, and calm spots that allow you to share in the moment with your date. When you pull over for lunch you socialize with the others on your trip, but make time to sneak off for a walk with your girl. A brief make-out session while you take turns peeing in the woods makes for good time spent together on a group trip. Just as you begin to dry off, it is back into the wild waters for the second half of the trip. When you arrive back at the cabin you watch the slide show of pictures taken during the experience. You and she change into dry clothes and prepare for the drive to the bead and breakfast.

While she is in the changing room you call ahead to the B&B to make sure that the room is set up with a bottle of wine from the local winery and the flowers are fresh and prepared. They say that it is all set for your arrival. The drive is a quiet one with the both of you tired from the vigorous activity of the rafting trip. You play one of her Spotify playlists and cruise through the countryside with the windows down taking in the scenery and warm air. When you arrive at the bed and breakfast she was dozing off in the passenger seat.

"We're here," you say as you gently touch her hair. She creeps out of the car and stretches as you pop the trunk.

The place looks just like it did online, an old wood floored home, exuding warmth and a grandma's house like comfort. The owner tells you about the structure, and what time breakfast is served. You are the only residents booked for the weekend. The bathroom is down the hallway from the room and you are relieved because that rafting lunch isn't agreeing with your stomach. When your girl goes into the room she lets out a sigh, and goes over to the fresh flowers. She inhales and turns to the table with the wine nestled into a basket with cheeses and crackers.

"What a great room!" she says as she reads the label on the bottle. "This is where we are going tomorrow right?"

"Yup, this place is perfect for our weekend."

She doesn't need to hear from you that the wine and the flowers are something that you set up on your own, and if she never finds out it will be ok too. Providing the details is essential but taking credit for the work is not necessary. The fact that they are there is enough to make an association between you and the positive feelings she has about smelling her favorite flowers and tasting a great bottle of wine. Share in her joys and she will see them as yours (yours and hers) not just her joys. The goal is to create "couple" memories that are positive. If she tells the story of the weekend to a friend they will hear we's instead of I's when she tells the tales and that is how the EGA implants you as the bearer of all good things.

If she happens to chat up the owner and she tells her about your calls to set up the room then that's ok. She will be impressed, but she is a smart girl and might just figure out that you put in some legwork because what are the odds of her favorite flowers being in the room, and a wine from the vineyard you are going to visit the next day? Give her some credit by not taking credit unless she directly asks. If she does ask, then play it off as ensuring that she was comfortable and showing that you care about her.

The rest of the day you lounge around the old home, taking a nap and cuddling together. The owner indulges you both with a home-cooked country dinner and you discuss local history and the good life. Returning to the room you open the wine and cheeses. While you drink you are asking questions of your girl about her vacations in the past with her family, bringing back good memories and sharing yours with her. As the wine bottle empties and your bellies fill up, you return to the bed. The fragrance from the flowers creeps into your nostrils and you can sense the moment is right to take the next step.

You have had a full day beginning with excitement and ending in leisure. With your bodies relaxed from the wine and your "couple comfort" as high as it has ever been, there is no better time to initiate a sexual experience. There are no distractions or wildlife to stop you tonight.

You tell your girl that you are going to take a shower, and you ask her to join you in the bathroom. She accepts the invitation. You start up the water and have a seat on a small bench in the room. She sits with you. You and her both disrobe and hop into the tub. You take turns washing each other. When the water is no longer steaming, you hop out and return to the bedroom. You lay her upon the bed, her robe barely coving her sensitivities. You gently rub her body all over from outside the robe, helping to dry her off and feeling the contours of her torso.

The old room is plenty warm, and you throw back the covers on the bed and move yourself up to the headboard. She scoots herself up to you as her robe falls slightly open. You pull her robe from her shoulders and bring the covers up around her bare body. She leans against you and you feel the softness of her breasts pressing against your chest. Discarding her robe to the floor and sliding out of yours, you align her underneath you, your legs to her side and you rise up to slide a pillow under her head.

You kiss her gently from the forehead down to the eyelids and nose, settling on her lips with a firm and long lock. Allowing time to catch your breath, you smile at her and ask her if she is confortable. She smiles and moans back, giving an accepting kiss in return. This is the moment; the work has been worth it. You have created a strong attraction, anticipation, and you have put in enough effort to feel emotionally invested in this woman.

You give soft breaths on her neck and ear as you whisper her how long you have wanted to feel her body and make love to her. Tell her that you had some fantasies about how this night might go down, and if she asks what they were, tell her that you pictured both of you using all of your body to make each other feel good. You then slowly creep down her neck to her sex-flushed chest. Give kisses and use the pads of your fingers to tease up the goose bumps to her skin. When you see that the skin is sensitive, give short hot circular breaths on the cool skin, with a dart of your tongue over the surface of her breasts, the sensation of hot/cold will keep her aroused and guessing what comes next.

Spend ample time caressing her breasts, but don't pay too much attention to the obvious. Go slow, and keep up the kissing along the way. When she is kissing you deeply in your mouth, she is ready for you to move your mouth to her areolas and nipples and then down her happy trail with quick kisses until you reach her vulva. Make yourself comfortable in your new home; go slower than you think you should with your mouth on both sides of her labia before you take slow laps with your tongue from the vagina up to the clitoris. You should look and feel like a dog drinking water. After some minutes with just a tongue, you can tease around her vagina with a finger as you tenderly circle or make letters around her clit. Take that index finger and insert it just barely palm down, twisting it upside down so you are now having your mouth on her clitoris and that finger is now pointing at your tongue from inside.

Keeping your mouth steady on he clit, you can slowly increase the tempo of your digit piston on the ceiling of her vagina. You want to be using the same motion you would to dig lint out of the bottom of a pocket, just inverted. When you feel her vagina slightly expand and it seems wet enough, you can experiment with a middle finger joining the party. If so, pull your index finger back to the opening and then barely insert the second finger, keeping both on the first inch inside her.

Gently press apart the fingers to give tension on the outer walls of her vagina, and move both fingers up to the knuckle back to the palms up position. You are now coaxing her orgasm from behind her cervix by motioning it to come closer to you, while having a steady pressure on the clit from above. Like watching the sunrise, you should be patient and comfortable as you can be.

You should be able to tell she is really getting into what you are doing. Listen to her body and you might even feel her cervix spasm just a bit as the pressure builds to an orgasm. Pay attention to her sounds and adjust to her movements. If she shuffles a bit, slow down or give less pressure with your mouth. If she pulls your hand, take out a finger or both, and come up to give her kisses. She might want to climax then or later, and you should not be finger blasting her or fighting her pussy like Wii boxing.

A gentleman is not preoccupied with orgasm. If it happens, great. If she wants to wait until you are inside her, then hopefully you have been masturbating for at least 15 minutes each time to build up better stamina. Use a rhythm method to track your pumps and to give yourself some variety. Use the 1-9, 2-8 pace. One deep pump, nine shallow pumps. Two deep pumps for eight shallow pumps. That should keep you enjoying different sensations and allow you to occupy your mind.

I find that if I can last two minutes, then I can last 50 if I had to. Drop a thumb down to her clit area for some extra friction, or move her hand to her vulva and see if she takes the bait. If she is comfortable, she will play with herself as you pump away. When you feel like coming, stop pumping. Relax and take some breaths. Pull her up to you so that you have your legs around each other. Sit like that and kiss deeply. As you recover, rock gently back and forth. It is a very intimate position, and you can compliment her on how sexy she looks.

Tell her to tell you how she wants you, and do as she wishes. When you are feeling too good, tell her that you are going to come soon. If there is no objection, feel free to get as dirty as you want for the next minute until you climax. Once you do, grab the base of the condom (you are wearing one right?) and slowly squeeze and pull out. Once out, tie it in a knot and excuse yourself briefly while you dispose of it in the bathroom trash. Don't wait too long to pull out, and don't ask to come on her face or tits. There will be other times to play show and tell with your sperm.

Return to her quickly and cuddle her while you gently caress her body. Have a water bottle or glass handy and offer her some. If you are not too eager, and you follow the plan, you guarantee a round two. You have just graduated with a PhD. in EGA. Hopefully you are happy with your partner and you leave the weekend as a couple instead of two individuals. After all, the EGA is a means to an end, and there is no better ending than a happy one.

Chapter Seven

Time to Go Mono

After a morning encore to the evening festivities, you can now brag to your friends that you have achieved the dream with your lady friend. The drive home is quiet and comfortable, no awkward silences, and hands are held over the shifter for most of the ride. As you near her home to drop her off, you want to tell her that you couldn't have had a better time with her, and that you want to show your commitment to her by being monogamous.

Tell her that you respect her ability to choose, and you understand if it feels sudden to her (it won't). If she gives an acknowledgement or agrees to do the same, give her the decency of asking her to be your girlfriend. It is a silly gesture for adults, but one that she will appreciate. It will be great marketing material for you with her girlfriends, and it is a guaranteed yes. You are not going to be losing anything by stating the obvious; you want to be with her.

You know you are lucky to be in this position, and it isn't worth giving up a sure and solid partner for the unknown or the strange, no matter how exotic it might seem. Even if it doesn't last very long, showing commitment is part of being a gentleman and being responsible for your actions. If you really feel the need to cheat in the future, just break up with her first. Being a serial dater is better than being a cheater.

You are now self-sufficient in finding a partner. I hope you have taken the decisions seriously, and taken some steps to improve your life while you have been reading the book. The important thing to remember is that improvement is ongoing. Getting a girl is not the same thing as keeping her. You created a contract when you got together, that you would at a minimum, keep up the standards that you have when you met.

You now have the tool belt for courtship; using the EGA will keep you in demand as a potential relationship partner. Have faith that you can put the lessons into practice. Dr. Ethan Gregory will return with another guide to maximize your potential in life and love. In the meantime, remember that you matter most!

Don't Stop Here!

Find more from Dr. Ethan Gregory

To see how Dr. Ethan Gregory guides the male readers on the path to finding you, read the "I'm Sorry, You are Not a Pick-Up Artist" book that is the other half of this collection. To receive the EGA in your inbox weekly, ask questions directly to Dr. G, and to see other Ethan Gregory projects, go to the official *You Matter Most!* website, www.drethangregory.com.

If you enjoyed the book, please leave a review on Amazon. Reviews make a huge difference to independent authors and the more reviews the book receives, the more exposure it will get online. It only takes a minute and would mean the world to him. Afterwards, Tell Dr. G. what you thought and like the Dr. Ethan Gregory Facebook page.

About the Author

Ethan Gregory began in the helping profession as a teenager, in AOL chat rooms giving advice to other teenagers and adults. His education in psychology, sexual health, dating, and parenting gives him a wide base of knowledge to help others. Providing social services, therapy, and school guidance honed his skills in mental health. He earned his doctoral degree in Counseling Psychology in 2014 from Argosy University, studying dating preferences. He has lived in America, China and Japan working as a counselor. He empowers his readers on an array of subject matters. Follow him on Twitter, @drethangregory.

You can contact/hire the hard working editor of this and other Dr.G works, Dawn Hanson, by email at dhanson@hotmail.com

www.ingramcontent.com/pod-product-compliance
Lightning Source LLC
Chambersburg PA
CBHW031405040426
42444CB00005B/420